The Thinkers' Guide to Life

edited by
Marilyn Mason

Marilyn Mason
The Thinkers' Guide to Life

First published in Great Britain in 2000

by

Rationalist Press Association
Bradlaugh House, 47 Theobald's Road, London, WC1X 8SP

© Marilyn Mason 2000

Printed by Butler and Tanner, Caxton Road,
Frome, Somerset BA11 1NF

Page design and layout
Shirley Dent

Cover design: *Thoughtprints*
from an original concept by
Marilyn Mason
designed by Nathan Parker

ISBN 0 301 00002 6

Do not fear god,
do not worry about
death; what is good
is easy to obtain,
what is terrible
can be endured.

Philodemus of Gadara (c110 - c40 BCE)

Thanks

to the following for their help and criticism:
Robert Ashby, Trevor Bamford,
Ellie Godson, Jim Herrick, Georgia Mason, Katy
Mason, Pat Nash, Florence Nash,
Claire Nobbs, Jonathan Newman,
Amber Ravenscroft;

and to Nigel Warburton
who introduced me to philosophy.

Foreword

This little book is a guide to living for thinkers, collected from some of the world's greatest thinkers and philosophers. Few, if any, of those quoted are religious in the sense of believing that gods or an afterlife have any part to play in our living the best possible lives. Their ideas are firmly based in human nature and experience, essentially humanist in their belief in the human capacity to question, reason and observe, and thus work out answers to life's problems. The somewhat eccentric arrangement of the quotations is deliberate - ideas are intended to flow and to relate to each other, and to you, across history, regardless of chronology. As in any dialogue, not everyone agrees, but I hope that you will find many ideas that support your thinking. Brief quotations can be memorable and accessible, but, inevitably, give an incomplete view of the thinking of these writers, so sources and dates (of works where possible, or of authors) have been given so that you can read further.

I hope that non-religious people and thoughtful sceptics especially will find reassurance and inspiration in the wisdom and benevolence of these thinkers from four millennia. It is a sad fact of history that the thoughts of men have been better recorded than those of women, but I hope that the 21st century will redress the balance.

Marilyn Mason

Acknowledgements

Every effort has been made to check references and to trace copyright holders of the quotations in this book. However, this has proved difficult in some cases and the publishers will be pleased to correct any oversights at the earliest opportunity. The following have given permission to use extracts:

Cambridge University Press: G E Moore *Principia Ethica*.
Constable & Robinson Publishing Ltd: George Santayana *Soliloquies in England*.
Richard Dawkins: *Unweaving the Rainbow* (Allen Lane / The Penguin Press, 1998).
Sigmund Freud © Copyrights, The Institute of Psychoanalysis and the **Hogarth Press**: *The Standard Edition of the Complete Psychological Works of Sigmund Freud* translated and edited by James Strachey.
Ludovic Kennedy: for an abridged version of sentences from *All In the Mind; A Farewell to God* (Hodder & Stoughton, 1999).
Alan Marshall: translation from Montaigne.
Melitta Mew: Karl Popper *The Open Society and its Enemies*.
Lois Mitchison: JBS Haldane *Possible Worlds*.
Penguin Books Ltd: Albert Camus *The Myth Of Sisyphus*, translated by Justine O'Brien (first published in France by Gallimard, 1942, Hamish Hamilton, 1955) English translation copyright © Justine O'Brien; Albert Camus *American Journals*, translated by Hugh Levick (Hamish Hamilton, 1989)
copyright © 1978 Editions Gallimard, © 1988 Paragon House (first English language edition.

Contents

Wear a smile and have friends;
wear a scowl and have
wrinkles.
What do we live for
if not to make the world
less difficult for each other?

Attributed to George Eliot / Mary Ann
Evans (1819 - 80)

The unexamined life is not worth living.

Socrates

from *Plato's Apology*, c375 BCE

The life of man is of no greater importance to the universe than that of an oyster.

David Hume (1711 - 1776)

Of Suicide

The value of life lies not in its length, but in the use we make of it.

Michel de Montaigne (1533 - 92)

Essays

Isn't it a noble, an enlightened way of spending our brief time in the sun, to work at understanding the universe and how we have come to wake up in it? This is how I answer when I am asked – as I am surprisingly often – why I bother to get up in the mornings. To put it the other way round, isn't it sad to go to your grave without wondering why you were born? Who, with such a thought, would not spring from bed eager to resume discovering the world and rejoicing to be part of it?

Richard Dawkins
Unweaving the Rainbow, 1998

By what combination of elements, or actions of forces, I came to be what I am, does not at all touch my personal complacency, or interfere with my awe of the universe.

Harriet Martineau

in *Letters on the Laws of Man's Nature and Development,* 1851

**I should say the
universe is just there,
and that is all.**

Bertrand Russell (1872 – 1970)

when asked in a radio debate how he
would explain the existence of the
universe.

There is no cure for
birth or death
save to enjoy the interval.

George Santayana

Soliloquies in England,
1914 - 18

Reason, Observation and
Experience
– the Holy Trinity of Science –
have taught us that
happiness is the only good;
that the time to be happy is
now, and the way to be happy
is to make others so.

Robert Green Ingersoll

The Gods, 1876

The happy life is to an extraordinary extent the same as the good life.

Bertrand Russell

The Conquest of Happiness, 1930

When people who are tolerably fortunate in their outward lot do not find in life sufficient enjoyment to make it valuable to them, the cause generally is, caring for nobody but themselves.

John Stuart Mill

Utilitarianism, 1863

The secret of happiness is this: let your interests be as wide as possible and let your reactions to the things and persons that interest you be as far as possible friendly rather than hostile.

Bertrand Russell

The Conquest of Happiness, 1930

... It only needs a little courage
to fulfil wishes
which have previously
been regarded as unattainable.

Sigmund Freud

The Interpretation of Dreams, 1900
(footnote added in 1909)

The secret
for harvesting from life
the greatest fruitfulness
and the greatest enjoyment is
- to live dangerously!
Build your cities on the slopes of
Vesuvius!
Send your ships into uncharted
seas!

Friedrich Nietzsche
The Gay Science, 1882

The main constituents
of a satisfied life
appear to be two,
either of which is often found
sufficient for the purpose:
tranquillity and excitement.

John Stuart Mill
Utilitarianism, 1863

It is necessary
to the happiness of man
that he be mentally faithful
to himself.
Infidelity does not consist
in believing,
or in disbelieving,
it consists
in professing to believe
what one does not believe.

Thomas Paine

The Age of Reason, 1794

The things you really need
are few and easy to come by;
but the things
you can imagine you need
are infinite,
and you will
never be satisfied.

Epicurus

Principle Doctrines, c300 BCE

How little is requisite to supply the necessities of nature? And in a view to pleasure, what comparison between the unbought satisfaction of conversation, society, study, even health and the common beauties of nature, but above all the peaceful reflection on one's own conduct; what comparison, I say, between these and the feverish, empty amusements of luxury and expense? These natural pleasures, indeed, are really without price; both because they are below all price in their attainment, and above it in their enjoyment.

David Hume

An Enquiry Concerning the Principles of Morals, 1751

**All my life through,
the new sights of Nature
made me rejoice like a child.**

Marie Curie (1867-1934)

Pierre Curie

... personal affections
and aesthetic enjoyments
include all the greatest,
and by far the greatest,
goods we can imagine ...

G E Moore

Principia Ethica, 1903

Since pleasure is our only good,
we do not choose
every pleasure thoughtlessly,
but will decline many pleasures
that are more trouble
than they are worth.

Epicurus

Letter to Menoeceus, **c300 BCE**

The happiness of a really good successful piece of difficult work is very, very great indeed, and I don't think that the lazy person ever experiences anything quite like it.

Attributed to Bertrand Russell (1872 - 1970)

Ask yourself if you are happy
and you cease to be so.

John Stuart Mill

Autobiography, 1873

Nothing in life is to be feared.
It is only to be understood.

Attributed to Marie Curie (1867 - 1934)

If one does not know
to which port one is sailing,
no wind is favourable.

Seneca (4 BCE - 65 CE)

It is only those who do nothing that make no mistakes.

Attributed to Joseph Conrad (1857 - 1924)

Someone who had the strength to be just a maker of plans all his life would be a very happy man; but he would occasionally have to take a rest from this activity by carrying out a plan – and then come the irritation and the sobering up.

Friedrich Nietzsche

Assorted Opinions and Maxims, 1886 (supplement to *Human, All Too Human,* 1878)

Whenever you have a mishap,
remember to ask yourself
how you can make use of it.

Epictetus
Handbook, 1st Century CE

Struggling against the noose
merely tightens it ...
The only relief
for insoluble problems
is to endure
and to yield to necessity.

Seneca (4 BCE - 65 CE)

De Ira

There is no sun without shadow,
and it is essential
to know the night.

Albert Camus
The Myth of Sisyphus, 1942

It is better to be a human being dissatisfied than a pig satisfied; better to be Socrates dissatisfied than a fool satisfied. And if the fool, or the pig, is of a different opinion, it is because they only know their side of the question.

John Stuart Mill
Utilitarianism, 1863

When making decisions,
we need to consider
our goals in life and the facts
that we know and experience;
everything else just creates
uncertainty and confusion.

Epicurus

Principal Doctrines, c300 BCE

Whatever does not kill me
makes me strong.

Friedrich Nietzsche
Twilight of the Idols, 1889

There is nothing dreadful
in life for those
who have truly understood
that there is nothing terrible
in not living.

Epicurus

Letter to Menoeceus,
c300 BCE

Do not do to others what you would not like for yourself.

Confucius

Analects, c500 BCE

... what is not possible
is not to choose.
I can always choose,
but I must know
that if I do not choose,
that is still a choice.

Jean-Paul Sartre
Existentialism and Humanism, **1946**

Actions are right in proportion as they tend to promote happiness, wrong as they tend to produce the reverse of happiness.

John Stuart Mill
Utilitarianism, 1863

Repay injury with justice,
and kindness with kindness.

Confucius
Analects, c500 BCE

Natural justice
guarantees mutual advantage,
preventing one
from harming others
and from being harmed.

Epicurus
Principle Doctrines, c300 BCE

Always treat people
as ends in themselves,
never as means to an end.

Immanuel Kant

Groundwork of the Metaphysics of Morals, 1785

... one ought always to ask oneself what would happen if everyone did as one is doing; nor can one escape from that disturbing thought except by a kind of self-deception.

Jean-Paul Sartre

Existentialism and Humanism, 1946

... virtue is attended by more peace of mind than vice, and meets with a more favourable reception from the world. I am sensible, that, according to the past experience of mankind, friendship is the chief joy of human life and moderation the only source of tranquillity and happiness.

David Hume

Enquiry Concerning Human Understanding, 1748

It is impossible for someone who secretly does something that mankind has agreed is harmful, to be confident that he will escape detection, even if he escapes it ten thousand times. Until he dies, he will always be uncertain of remaining undetected.

Epicurus

Principle Doctrines, c300 BCE

It is impossible to live
pleasantly without living
wisely, virtuously and justly,
just as we cannot live
wisely, virtuously and justly
without living pleasantly.

Epicurus

Letter to Menoeceus, c300 BCE

I do not like negative virtues –
virtues whose very essence is
to negate and deny oneself
something.

Friedrich Nietzsche

The Gay Science,1882

Just as the sun does not wait for prayers and incantations to persuade it to rise, but shines anyway and is universally loved, so you should not wait for applause and praise in order to do good; but be a voluntary benefactor and you will be beloved like the sun.

Epictetus

Handbook, 1st Century CE

There is only one good,
knowledge;
there is only one evil,
ignorance.

Socrates

Epigrams, c400 BCE

Honest people
have most peace of mind;
dishonest people
are full of worries and fears.

Epicurus

Principle Doctrines, c300 BCE

**Conformity to nature
has no connection whatever
with right and wrong.**

John Stuart Mill

On Nature, 1874

As man advances in civilisation, and small tribes are united into larger communities, the simplest reason would tell each individual that he ought to extend his social instincts and sympathies to all the members of the same nation, though personally unknown to him. This point once reached, there is only an artificial barrier to prevent his sympathies extending to the men of all nations and races.

Charles Darwin

The Descent of Man, 1871

It is not the fault of any creed, but of the complicated nature of human affairs, that rules of conduct cannot be so framed as to require no exception, and that hardly any action can be safely laid down as either always obligatory or always condemnable.

John Stuart Mill

Utilitarianism, 1863

God, Immortality, Duty...
how inconceivable the first,
how unbelievable the second,
and yet how peremptory and
absolute the third.

George Eliot / Mary Ann Evans

in conversation with FWH Myers,
reported in *Century* magazine, 1881

The only possible basis for a sound morality is mutual tolerance and respect: tolerance of one another's customs and opinions; respect for one another's rights and feelings; awareness of one another's needs.

A J Ayer

The Humanist Outlook, 1968

The sympathies of our nature are strengthened by pondering cogitations, and deadened by thoughtless use. Macbeth's heart smote him more for one murder, the first, than for a hundred subsequent ones, which were necessary to back it.

Mary Wollstonecraft

A Vindication of the Rights of Women, 1792

If the capacity for evil
is part of human nature,
so is the capacity for good.

A J Ayer,

The Humanist Outlook, 1968

Tolerance,
good temper and sympathy –
they are what matter really,
and if the human race
is not to collapse
they must come to the front
before long.

EM Forster

What I Believe, 1938

'Tis one thing to know virtue,
and another
to conform the will to it.

David Hume

A Treatise of Human Nature, 1740

Of all the means
by which wisdom ensures
happiness throughout life,
by far the most important
is the possession of friendship.

Epicurus

Principle Doctrines, c300 BCE

It is not so much
our friends' help that we need,
as the confident knowledge
that they will help us.

Epicurus

Fragments, c300 BCE

The mere fact of their common humanity requires that one man should feel another to be kin to him.

Cicero

De Finibus, c44 BCE

People exist for each other.
So either improve them
or put up with them.

Marcus Aurelius (121 – 80 CE)

Meditations

We ought to be tolerant
of each other,
because we are all
weak, inconsistent, and
liable to fickleness and mistakes.

Voltaire,

Philosophical Dictionary, 1764

We should be bound by the
laws of humanity to give gentle
usage to these creatures.

David Hume,

*An Enquiry Concerning the Principles of
Morals*, 1752

The question is not,
Can they reason?
nor Can they talk?
but Can they suffer?

Jeremy Bentham

*Introduction to the Principles of Morals
and Legislation,* 1789

We know but little of the powers and experience of brutes, even as the dog knows little of the experience of the cat, or the bird that of the frog: but what we know indicates consciousness as clearly as sentience.

Harriet Martineau

in *Letters on the Laws of Man's Nature and Development,* 1851

By liberty, then, we can only mean a power of acting or not acting, according to the determinations of the will; that is, if we choose to remain at rest, we may; if we choose to move, we also may.

David Hume

Enquiry Concerning Human Understanding, 1748

Are we like the leaf
blowing in the autumn winds,
saying to itself,
"Now I'll go this way,
now I'll go that. "?

Attributed to Ludwig Wittgenstein (1889 -1951)

All oppression
creates a state of war.

Simone de Beauvoir

The Second Sex, 1949

Whatever crushes individuality is despotism.

John Stuart Mill

On Liberty, 1859

The only purpose for which power can rightfully be exercised over any member of a civilised community, against his will, is to prevent harm to others.

John Stuart Mill

On Liberty, 1859

Whoever, then, wants to be free,
let him never want anything
nor avoid anything,
which depends on others.

Epictetus

Handbook, c100CE

No bad man is free ...
Only the educated are free.

Epictetus

Discourses, **c100CE**

As it is useful that while mankind are imperfect there should be different opinions; so it is that there should be different experiments in living.

John Stuart Mill

On Liberty, 1859

No one was ever injured
by the truth;
but he who persists
in self-deception and ignorance
is injured.

Marcus Aurelius (121 – 80 CE)
Meditations

The wisest is he who realises,
like Socrates,
that in respect of wisdom
he knows nothing.

Plato

Apology, **c375 BCE**

Only when we know little
can we be certain;
doubt grows
with greater learning.

Goethe (1749 - 1832)

Sprüche Prosa

A wise man proportions his belief to the evidence.

David Hume

An Enquiry Concerning Human Understanding, 1748

**We are like sailors
who in the open sea
must reconstruct their ship
but are never able
to start afresh
from the bottom
or with the best materials.**

Otto Neurath (1882 - 1945)

Protocol Sentences

My own suspicion is that
the universe is not only queerer
than we suppose,
but queerer than
we *can* suppose.

J B S Haldane

Possible Worlds, 1927

Weakness, fear, melancholy,
together with ignorance,
are ... the true sources
of superstition.

David Hume

Of Superstition and Enthusiasm, 1741

It is wrong for a man to say that he is certain of the objective truth of any proposition unless he can produce evidence which logically justifies that certainty.

T H Huxley

Agnosticism and Christianity, **1889**

Rationalism is an attitude of readiness to listen to contrary arguments and to learn from experience ... of admitting that "I may be wrong and you may be right and, by an effort, we may get nearer the truth."

Karl Popper

The Open Society and its Enemies, 1945

What we cannot speak about
we must pass over in silence.

Ludwig Wittgenstein

Tractatus, 1921

About the gods, I am unable to know whether they exist or do not exist, nor what they are like in form: for there are things that hinder sure knowledge – the obscurity of the subject and the shortness of human life.

Protagoras (482 - 414 BCE)

God is a hypothesis,
and, as such,
stands in need of proof;
the onus probandi
[burden of proof]
rests on the theist.

Percy Bysshe Shelley

Note on Queen Mab; a Philosophical Poem, 1813

Fear is the main source
of superstition and one of
the main sources of cruelty.
To conquer fear
is the beginning of wisdom.

Bertrand Russell

An Outline of Intellectual Rubbish, in
Unpopular Essays, 1950

If the gods have the will to remove evil and cannot, then they are not all-powerful. If they are neither able nor willing, they are neither all-powerful or benevolent. If they are both able and willing to annihilate evil, why does it exist?

Epicurus, c300 BCE

... it is better to love men
than to fear gods ...
it is grander and nobler
to think and investigate
for yourself
than to repeat a creed ...

Robert Green Ingersoll

The Gods, 1876

Religion ...
is the opium of the people ...
To abolish religion
as the illusory happiness
of the people
is to demand their
real happiness.

Karl Marx (1818 -1883)

*Towards a Critique of Hegel's Philosophy
of Right*

The established churches have hijacked human altruism, common to all people of all times, of all religions and none, and called it "Christian values".

Ludovic Kennedy

All In the Mind; A Farewell to God, 1999

In the long run, nothing can withstand reason and experience, and the contradiction religion offers to both is only too palpable.

Sigmund Freud

The Future of an Illusion, 1937

**Faith: a firm belief
for which there is no evidence.**

Bertrand Russell

Human Society in Ethics and Politics,
1954

When I ceased to accept the teaching of my youth, it was not so much a process of giving up beliefs, as of discovering that I had never really believed.

Leslie Stephen

The Aims of Ethical Societies, 1900

**My country is the world,
and my religion is to do good.**

Thomas Paine

The Rights of Man, 1791

... When I enter most intimately into what I call myself, I always stumble on some particular perception or other, of heat or cold, light or shade, love or hatred, pain or pleasure. I can never catch myself at any time without a perception, and can never observe anything but the perception.

David Hume

A Treatise of Human Nature, 1748

Man is nothing else
but what he purposes ...
he is nothing else
but the sum of his actions,
nothing else but what his life is.

Jean-Paul Sartre

Existentialism and Humanism, 1946

The true ground of awe is in finding ourselves what we are; not in dreams of how we came to be what we are ... We are what we are, however we came to be ...

Harriet Martineau

in *Letters on the Laws of Man's Nature and Development*, 1851

Character is fate.

Novalis (1772-1801)

quoted by Thomas Hardy in *The Mayor of Casterbridge*, 1886

A tree
cannot exist high in the air,
or clouds
in the depths of the sea,
and fish
cannot live in the fields
or blood flow in wood
or sap in stones...
so the mind cannot exist
without a body
or apart from sinews and blood

Lucretius (c95 - 55 BCE)

On the Nature of the Universe

Transience value
is scarcity value in time.
Limiting the possibility
of an enjoyment
raises the value of the
enjoyment.

Sigmund Freud

On Transience, 1916

Unlimited time and limited
time give the same quantity
of pleasure,
if we understand
the limits of pleasure correctly.

Epicurus,

Principal Doctrines, c300 BCE

To cease to love and be lovable
is a death unbearable;
to cease to live is nothing.

Voltaire (1694 – 1778)

poem to Mme de Châtelet

I was not –
I was –
I am not –
I do not mind.

Epicurean epitaph, used from c300 BCE

Death is nothing to us: for after our bodies have been dissolved by death they are without sensation, and that which lacks sensation is nothing to us. And therefore a right understanding of death makes mortality enjoyable, not because it adds to an infinite span of time, but because it takes away the craving for immortality.

Epicurus

Principal Doctrines, c300 BCE

The old must always
make way for the new,
and one thing must be built
out of the ruins of another.
There is no murky pit of hell
awaiting anyone.

Lucretius (c95 - 55 BCE)

On the Nature of the Universe

In a little while
you will be no one and nowhere,
and everything around you
and everyone who is now alive
will exist no more.
Nature's law is that everything
changes and passes,
so that, in due course,
other things may come to exist.

Marcus Aurelius (121 – 80 CE)

Meditations

Be sure, then,
that we have nothing to fear
in death.
Someone who no longer exists
cannot suffer,
or differ in any way
from someone
who has not been born.

Lucretius (c95 - 55 BCE)
On the Nature of the Universe

..the desire of an indefinite prolongation of existence is believed by many to be in itself sufficient proof of the reality of a future life.

John Stuart Mill
On Nature, 1874

The wise man neither rejects life nor fears death ... just as he does not necessarily choose the largest amount of food, but, rather, the pleasantest food, so he prefers not the longest time, but the most pleasant.

Epicurus

Letter to Menoeceus, C300 BCE

I cannot conceive of a god who rewards and punishes his creatures or has a will of the kind that we experience ourselves. Neither can I nor would I want to conceive of an individual that survives his physical death; let feeble souls, from fear or absurd egoism, cherish such thoughts.

Albert Einstein

The World As I See It, 1934

Against everything else
it is possible
to make oneself safe;
but in the case of death,
we all live in an unfortified city.

Epicurus

Vatican Sayings, c300 BCE

The world is so exquisite, with so much love and moral depth, that there is no reason to deceive ourselves with pretty stories for which there's little good evidence. Far better, it seems to me, in our vulnerability, is to look Death in the eye and to be grateful every day for the brief but magnificent opportunity that life provides.

Carl Sagan

Billions and Billions, 1997

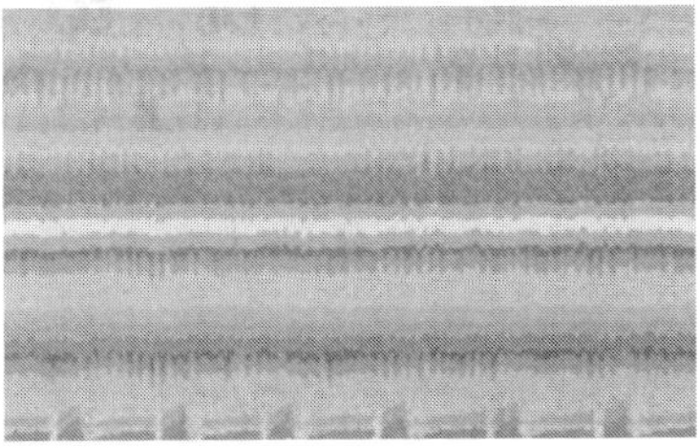

If you enjoyed sharing these ideas and would
like to find out more about humanist thinking,
contact the Rationalist Press Association, which
published this book, or the British Humanist
Association. The BHA exists to enable non-
religious people to live their lives with
confidence and integrity, by providing advice,
helping with non-religious ceremonies, and
publicly representing their philosophy and
ethical concerns.

RPA, 47 Theobalds Road, London WC1X 8SP
020 7430 1371
www.rationalist.org.uk
BHA, 47 Theobalds Road, London WC1X 8SP
020 7430 0908
www.humanism.org.uk